To: Amber
From: Grandma C

M000032612

Thursdays with Naomi

Stand Still and Look

Until You Really See

Phillip Thorne

Illustrations by Sarahbeth

Published by Wingspread Publishers, Camp Hill, Pennsylvania.
www.wingspreadpublishers.com. A division of Zur Ltd.

ISBN: 978-1-60066-342-0

Cover: Jared Reneker
Illustrations: Sarahbeth Thorne

For Rachel

Thursdays with Naomi

Contents

"So often people say we should look to the elderly, learn from their wisdom, their many years. I disagree. I say we should look to the young: untarnished, without stereotypes implanted in their minds, no poison, no hatred in their hearts. When we learn to see life through the eyes of a child that is when we become truly wise."

Mother Teresa

Introduction

"Too soon oldt undt too late schmart"

It must have been more than thirty years ago, long before my granddaughter, Naomi, was born. My wife and I were browsing through an old curiosity shop on Highway 30, near Amish country in south central Pennsylvania, and there it was, painted in small black letters on an iron trivet. I remember it was a trivet because I had to ask my wife what it was, and when she told me, I still didn't know. I had never heard the word trivet before. But there on this trivet were the words, *Ve get too soon oldt undt too late schmart.*

I wish I had bought that bit of cornball, but I was too young at the time to appreciate the wisdom. I just laughed and moved on. But when the idea for this book dawned on me that long forgotten saying echoed in my mind, for this book and that trivet were born from the same all-too-common experience. When we finally learn the lessons life has to teach we wonder, "Why did it take so long?"

There is an irony at the heart of the book you hold in your hands. I am finally old enough to have a granddaughter, which means I now laugh at *myself* when I think of someone *too soon oldt*. But the irony is that the *schmarts* I hope to share is the wisdom I have found contemplating the simple words and deeds of a not-yet-three-year-old child.

I guess that's the way things are. It takes years to learn how to listen, and it takes someone you love more than words can say to help you slow down enough to see what has been there all along. Or perhaps wisdom comes from a lifetime of experience seen through the eyes of a child.

Of course, if I were a better disciple of Jesus, I might have learned all these things sooner. Didn't he tell us two thousand years ago that the kingdom of heaven belongs to such as these, referring to children, and that we must become like little children if we ever hope to enter that kingdom? But alas, *ve get too soon oldt undt too late schmart.*

Chapter One

"I'm Sorry Gramps"

Some things in life just have to be experienced, like the smell of bread baking in the oven, or the feeling of falling in love. So when some star struck person with graying hair tells you what it is like to be a grandparent, just take his word for it. It won't do any good to doubt him anyway. For me, becoming a grandfather was like falling in love all over again. Not at first sight, mind you; it was more gradual than that. But somewhere between the first look and the first word she spoke, my granddaughter, Naomi, became one of the great loves of my life.

So it will come as no great surprise that Thursday is now the most anticipated day in every fortnight, for that is the time when Naomi comes to spend the day with her MiMi and Gramps. By the end of it we drop into our recliners exhausted from the day's activities— tracing numbers in the counting book, building a 'garage' for baby with blocks, drawing crayon hearts, or reading the adventures of Frog and Toad for the umpteenth time. "Again, again" Naomi says. "Do it again." Of course MiMi and Gramps do it again (and again and again).

No matter how much we enjoy the day (and we do), MiMi and Gramps are always happy to say goodnight and walk downstairs to pour that long awaited glass of wine. But first we have to put our precious visitor to bed. As you might imagine, there is a preparation ritual for that, because children love rituals and also, once you start a ritual (which we have) it is really hard to stop.

So our ritual begins with a bath, and not just any bath. Captain Michael and his singing tugboat need to be in the bath, along with a little rubber duck and lots of bubbles. There has to be playing and splashing and yes, eventually, bathing. Then when the bath is over, Gramps lifts Naomi out of the tub and lays her down in a soft, warm towel to dry. After plenty of hugs and kisses, it is time to dress for bed, which begins with the night time diaper.

Unfortunately, our little angel has just recently developed a habit of resisting the diaper. She twists and turns and arches her back, with a mischievous little smile on her face, occasionally looking our way to see how we are responding. So one night not too long ago, after gently wrestling with her for a while, I finally stopped in frustration and said in a rather stern voice, "Naomi, you are being very difficult for Gramps!"

She paused and lay still, and for a fleeting moment I worried that I had spoken too harshly. But then Naomi looked me in the eyes and softly said, "I'm sorry, Gramps."

I melted.

So quickly, so sincerely, so disarmingly, Naomi heard what I said, considered the situation and repented. She changed her mind and sealed the change with the most adorable "I'm sorry, Gramps" you will ever hear. I wondered, "Will she keep that tender heart forever?"

I also wondered why we grownups find it so hard to say "I'm sorry" (or should I say, *this* grown up). The very week Naomi opened the windows of my heart with her sweet little "I'm sorry," I had shut the door to my wife's by failing to apologize. It wasn't the first time, either.

What is it about those three little words that make them so hard to say—and so powerful when we finally say them? Perhaps it is the change of heart that must take place before we say them. Think about it. In order to sincerely say "I'm sorry," a person must stop asserting and defending long enough to look, through a deliberate act of sympathetic insight, into the heart of another. It is only when I see what another person sees and, in some sense feel what she feels, that I become genuinely sorry for what I have done. Without that moment of empathy we never really feel sorry, and even if we say the words, they do not ring true.

But when empathetic insight is genuinely expressed it has the power to melt a human heart. We have all experienced it. We all know how good it feels to be understood. That's the power of the bond between true friends, and why not feeling understood by someone we love is so hurtful. When a person we love fails to say "I'm sorry," we experience it as a failure to understand, or even worse, a refusal to care enough to listen to what we are saying. "If only he would listen, he would understand! And if he really loved me, he would listen."

Of course, saying "I'm sorry" is not just saying "I understand." It is also saying "I did it." It is taking responsibility for the pain the other person is experiencing. As much as we hate to admit it, there is something in us that does not want to acknowledge fault. We would rather explain ourselves or defend ourselves. "No, I didn't do that," or "I didn't mean to do it," or "I didn't mean by doing it what you thought I meant." In other words, "It was not really my fault and if you would only look at the situation differently you wouldn't be so hurt." Then, if explaining or defending does not work, we counter attack. "Well, you did this and that, and those things were worse than anything I did." We twist and turn, block and jab, raising our voices and inflicting more wounds in the process.

All we really need to do is stop, look the other person in the heart, and say "I'm sorry, Gramps" or "I'm sorry, Hon" or "I'm sorry, Dear Friend." Am I oversimplifying? Is it unfair to reduce the complexities of human conflict to the confessions of a little child? Perhaps. But after years of reflection on my own experience and that of others, I really do not think so. The basic source of conflict between family and friends (not to mention acquaintances and enemies) is selfishness and pride. I am too self-centered to look the other person in the heart and see what the world looks like from her perspective, and I am too proud to admit that the problems between us are as much my fault as anyone's. In other words, I am too proud to humble myself like a little child.

Now I do not for a moment think Naomi understood these things when she looked in my eyes and with that sweet little voice said, "I'm sorry, Gramps." I imagine she simply experienced a natural intuitive insight into my frustration and displeasure with her actions. Perhaps she felt guilty as well. But mostly she didn't want Gramps to be unhappy with her. She loves Gramps and she loves being loved by Gramps, and the feeling of my displeasure was not worth whatever pleasure she was experiencing from resisting the diaper.

If she were older she probably could have explained herself. "Gramps, I'm just playing.

Don't be mad." Or, "Gramps, I don't want to go to bed. That's why I'm twisting and turning." Or maybe, "Gramps, I think what is really happening is that I have an unconscious feeling it is time for me to stop wearing diapers." Fortunately, Naomi has not yet advanced to these stages of explanation.

Wouldn't it be nice if she never did? And wouldn't the world be a better place if grown-ups like you and I simply learned to say, "I'm sorry," with the empathy and humility of a little child?

Perhaps I should go talk to my wife...

Chapter Two

"Again, Again"

I must have been fourteen when a troupe of traveling dramatists came to town to perform a musical in our church and sang a chorus which has always stuck with me. It had a catchy tune and a rhythmic beat, but I am sure I remembered it because of the strobe lights. During the verses of the song the actors and actresses would move about on stage. Then suddenly, as the lights began to strobe, they would freeze, and in a pulsating beat chant these haunting words: "Always in a hurry, always in hurry, always in hurry day and night; always in hurry, always in a hurry, always in a hurry the story of my life."

I guess even then I sensed something was wrong. At the ripe old age of fourteen I felt like the song was about me. I was the one always in a hurry—rushing to class, to practice, to church, to home and back again. I had absorbed, almost unconsciously, the race for achievement which had become the drumbeat of my surrounding culture. Since I was good at it—hurried achievement, that is—I was rewarded. I was rewarded with good grades, high honors, popularity and the pressure to keep hurrying.

I have another childhood memory. This one is a poster hanging on the wall in my sister's room. It was printed in rather drab, sepia tones, and the picture itself was not that captivating: a solitary individual standing at dusk in a field of brown flowers, each one very much like the other, with one exception. All by itself, not far from the lone observer, was a single spot of color in an otherwise colorless world. One flower printed in orange. The caption at the bottom said it all: "Stand still and look until you really see." I think my sister's poster stuck with me for the same reason the childhood chorus did. I never stood still long enough to see much of anything. I was always in a hurry, always in a hurry, day and night.

But something happens when a man in a hurry reaches middle age. Actually, several things happen all at once. The body slows down and the energy levels decrease to the point where it becomes harder and harder to be in a hurry day and night. Then the mind begins to question the point of it all. Where am I going in such a hurry, anyway? If that were not enough, in the midst of these bodily changes and mental ponderings, I became a grandparent. Arriving at a place in life where I could actually see the end of the road, and ponder paths not taken, I received the gift of contemplating the beginning all over again through the eyes of a child.

If I were to pick one thing Naomi has said during our Thursdays together that means more to me than all the other cute and clever, wise and wonderful things she says, it would have to be, "Again, again." It may also be the words she speaks more than any other. We read a story, Naomi says, "Again, again." We play Hide and Seek, she says, "Again, again." We lift her above our heads and swing her around, we make funny faces in the restaurant, we tickle her tummy, we sing a song, we dance a jig, we build a tower with blocks and knock it down, and Naomi says to MiMi and Gramps, "Again, again." Lift me up again, tickle me again, sing again, build the tower again so I can knock it down all over again.

At first, this "Again, again" was cute, probably because I find almost anything my granddaughter does cute at first. But soon I found myself trying to talk her out of it. "Let's do this, instead," I would say. Or, "Why don't we do something else now?" The truth is, I was bored. Once was enough for me, maybe twice was all right. But over and over again— where is the pleasure in that?

But Naomi was finding pleasure in it, so much pleasure that she was quite happy to do it again. In fact, every time she experienced whatever we were doing she seemed to find pleasure in it. I, on the other hand, lost interest rather quickly. I wanted to move on to the next thing. I was in a hurry.

So I began to wonder: What was it that made Naomi's experience so different from mine? Was I missing something? Soon I began to ask other questions. Why did I want to stop blowing bubbles, anyway? Were the bubbles any less graceful as they floated up, up and away a second and a third time? Was Naomi's giggle at our butterfly kisses any less joyful because it happened again and again? Was the wisdom of Frog and Toad less insightful just because I had heard the story for the umpteenth time? Finally, if those things were beginning to feel less beautiful and joyful and wise, why in the world would that be?

Eventually it dawned on me: I *was* missing something, something very precious, and I had probably been missing it most of my life (at least since I was fourteen): that wonderful child-like capacity to enjoy the pleasures of the present moment, especially the real and deep pleasures of love shared.

G.K. Chesterton once suggested, in his classic little book *Orthodoxy*, that it is perhaps this capacity to find pleasure in doing the same thing over and over again that makes children more like God than their parents. Children have "abounding vitality," he wrote. They are full of life and they never tire of repetition. They experience the joy of each and every thing in each and every moment. So, too, does God. In fact, Chesterton mused,

It is possible that God says every morning, "Do it again" to the sun; and every evening, "Do it again" to the moon. It may not be automatic necessity that makes all daisies alike, it may be that God makes every daisy separately, but has never got tired of making them.

Even if that is not quite true as an explanation of origins, it expresses a deep moral truth. Every good thing is to be enjoyed, and one way of enjoying it fully is relishing its repetition. Perhaps we fallen creatures tire of repetition because we lose the taste for what is good in each and every moment.

At least I do; and I do so, most often, because I am on to the next thing, or at least, the idea of the next thing. The surprising truth, though, is that the present moment is where joy is found, because, strictly speaking, the present is all we have. The future is not yet, and the past has ceased to be. One cannot enjoy what is coming until it comes, and we find pleasure in the past only by means of memory—that is, by bringing what no longer exists into the present through imagination.

Perhaps I wax too philosophical. So let me be practical: By entering into the joy of repetition with my granddaughter, I am finally learning to stand still and look until I really see. What is more, I am not just learning to savor butterfly kisses and bubbles in Naomi's presence. I am also learning to savor sunrises and sunsets even when she is gone. Not that I have never done so. But I am being disciplined, if you will, by the practice of doing it "again, again" to pay attention to the present moment and to find more pleasure in it.

So now when my wife and I sit down early in the morning to watch the sun rise, I sometimes think of Naomi. Then I smell the rich aroma of the coffee brewing and let it linger in my mind. I take a longer than usual look at the gently aging beauty of my bride of thirty-five years, and listen more intently to her heart. Then we watch in silent wonder the shifting color of the clouds as God says to the sun, "Do it again. Do it again."

Chapter Three

"Mommy Hug"

While living in Denver during our twenties, Cindi and I became good friends with two young couples. We even began to meet regularly as a small group, sharing hours of deep and engaging conversation. So we got to know each other quite well, and since one of the men was a psychologist he probably got to know the rest of us even better. Then one evening my psychologist friend gave me a gift. It was a little book with a picture on the cover of two cartoon bears hugging each other. The title was printed in clear letters above them: "Hug Therapy." We all laughed out loud, because everyone knew that book was written for me.

From my earliest years I have been less than comfortable with physical contact. I happened to grow up in a family that did not do much hugging, and that was all right by me. Then I met my wife, and her family hugged every chance they got. They hugged hello and they hugged goodbye. They hugged goodnight and good morning. They hugged when they gave each other presents and sometimes they even hugged for no good reason at all. So I had a problem.

Fortunately, I have learned over the years to give and receive physical affection more readily and easily than I once did. Being the only guy in a family of girls has certainly helped, as has celebrating holidays with my wife's hugging relatives. But I am still somewhat reserved (just ask my relatives) and earlier in our marriage I must have been even more so; hence, the gentle suggestion of my psychologist friend.

Well, Thursdays with Naomi have been the middle-aged equivalent of receiving a real life book on Hug Therapy. Not that Naomi is constantly hugging, because she is not. She has inherited a more reserved personality than her little brother, who is glad to go from one set of arms to another all day long. Naomi, on the other hand, is an introvert with a definite sense of personal space. But she also knows how to ask for a hug.

In fact, some of her earliest words were "Hug, hug." All of sudden she would look your direction, hold up her little arms and say "Hug." Sometimes all she meant was, "I want you to pick me up so I can see something up there," or "I want you to pick me up so I don't have to walk anymore." That is, it was equivalent to "Pick me up, please." But not always. Sometimes she meant "I want you to hold me close."

That is especially true when Naomi is frightened or hurt, or when she is feeling insecure or out of control. When that happens Naomi doesn't just say "Hug." She usually says, with some urgency, "Mommy, hug. Mommy, hug." And when Naomi calls for Mommy to pick her up and hold her tight, only Mommy will do. No one else—not even Gramps, I am sorry to say—will satisfy the cry of her little heart, because no one feels as safe, and no one makes her feel quite as understood as her Mommy.

When Naomi's mother was a little girl and we were trying to figure out how to do this impossible thing called parenting, we happened upon a book by Ross Campbell entitled, *How to Really Love Your Child.* What a gift! That book cut through the jungle of parenting challenges and competing opinions and offered a clear and simple strategy for creating a loving environment in which to nurture and train your children. Yes, children need discipline, Campbell acknowledges. They need to be trained and taught in a clear and consistent manner. But if that discipline is to be effective and the training is to take hold, then children must grow up in an environment of love. Love must be the soil and the sun of their lives.

But how do you really love your child—not just feel love for your child, but express it in such a way that your child feels loved? You do three basic things, Dr. Campbell suggests. You make repeated eye contact, reach out with physical touch and give your child focused personal attention. Eye contact, physical touch and focused attention—those three things, liberally and consistently given, will create an environment of love that serves as the soil and sun for a child's growing soul. Or, as Dr. Campbell sometimes puts it, these three actions will keep their emotional tanks running on full.

I, for one, must wholeheartedly agree. In fact I have come to believe that this simple, threefold strategy is some of the wisest advice we ever received.

But it is not just advice for children, is it? We do not stop needing our emotional tanks filled upon reaching adulthood, nor have those tanks formed walls so thick that, once filled, they never leak. No, adults still want and need affection, and when we do not receive it, everything else just seems more difficult. It is like running on empty.

When I come up behind my wife and begin to rub her shoulders, I not only feel the tension escaping, I can almost hear her emotional tank filling as she breathes more deeply. When I give her a gentle, lingering hug (with no thought of what I might receive in return), her response is like a child snuggling into my lap or a flower opening to the sun, maybe both at once. I have yet to hear of a better method for filling the emotional tank of someone you love than Ross Campbell's three simple acts: physical touch, eye contact and focused attention, often expressed as we grow older through heartfelt conversation.

One of my favorite personal snapshots is a picture of me and my twenty-something daughter, Sarah, sitting on a couch together. She is leaning back on my shoulder, with my arm around her, both of us wearing unmistakable smiles of contentment. If this picture were a poster, I would write across the top, "It doesn't get any better than this."

My daughter needs hugs. My wife needs hugs. My granddaughter and grandson need hugs. We all need hugs. I just wish we were as free to ask for them and give them as Naomi and her mother seem to be. Perhaps we wouldn't walk around with an empty emotional tank as often as we do.

Chapter Four

"Go Gramps, Go!"

I was tired. That's what happens when a middle-aged man spends the day playing with his granddaughter. It is also what happens when a man in a hurry lets the discipline of exercise slip from his life. So lifting myself slowly from the recliner where I had momentarily fallen for a rest, I decided to go downstairs and get on the treadmill. Perhaps this would be the first day of the rest of my exercising life.

Of course Naomi insisted upon going with me, and bringing MiMi along, too. While the two of them were playing on the floor I turned the machine on and began a brisk walk. A little way into the routine I was feeling fairly good, so I decided to pick up the pace and jog for a while, which for some reason caught

Naomi's attention. Perhaps it was all the huffing and puffing or the pounding of my heavy feet. But whatever it was, Naomi looked up, rose from her play and came over to where Gramps was making all that noise. Then with that darling voice of hers she started chanting, "Go Gramps, Go! Go Gramps, Go!"

A moment later, perhaps when she noticed the sweat dripping down my face, she added, "You can do it! You can do it!" For the next twenty minutes Naomi became my personal cheerleader, encouraging me with all the enthusiasm of someone watching the Olympic Games. Needless to say I kept running. I didn't drop the pace and start walking again, nor did I feel quite as tired. In fact, I felt strangely borne along by the earnest enthusiasm of my new-found fan.

I wish MiMi and Gramps could take credit for this spontaneous outburst of encouragement, but when we talked about it later we could not remember a single time in her short two and a half years when either of us had said, "Go Naomi, Go." Then I remembered, years ago, standing on a cross country course at my daughter's High School, shouting words of encouragement as she ran by.

Cross country is a lonely sport. The fans are few and the course is long, and the contest is won or lost by a runner's ability to push herself to the limit. So it really helps when someone is on the sideline cheering you on. I should know; it was my sport in school and it turned out to be the sport in which both my daughters chose to compete. So Naomi's mom was one of those weary runners I pushed along so many years ago. "Go Rachel, Go!" I shouted. "You can do it!"

Apparently encouragement is contagious. Children catch it from their parents, and then they pass it on to their children. Sometimes, if you are lucky, those children's children turn around and even encourage their grand-parents. "Go Gramps, Go!" Naomi shouted, and I heard an echo.

Actually, to be fair I heard the echo of Naomi's great-grandmother as well. It has been almost fifty years now, but I can still remember my mother reading to her children. She would read to us before we went to bed; she would read to us during the day; she even read to us while we were driving to Grandma and Grandpa's house for vacation. Of all the books I remember her reading, though, one is more memorable than the others. I cannot say it was because she read that book more often. I doubt she did. But that book was the one that stuck in my young mind.

It was the story of a little train engine that faced the challenge of pulling its cargo up an impossible hill. But what I remember most clearly about the story is the words the little engine chanted as it strained and struggled with its heavy load. "I think I can, I think I can, I think I can," it said with every puff of steam. In the end it did, which is why the book was called *The Little Engine That Could.*

That book was not just a story my mother read. It was a message she lived. In a hundred little ways she managed to communicate to her children that we could. We could overcome obstacles. We could accomplish things. We could live happy and rewarding lives.

To encourage is to give courage. It is not just to lift someone's spirits, but to inspire them to take action—to keep going when they feel like stopping, to take risks when they are afraid, to believe in themselves when others doubt them. Perhaps the most encouraging thing one person can do for another is to

believe in him; the second is to express that confidence in word and deed.

Cindi and I were far from perfect parents, but apparently we did one thing right. We believed in our children's abilities and spoke words of encouragement to them. We looked for things they did well and encouraged them to keep doing those things, and when their spirits flagged we sought to inspire them with enthusiastic support.

We had not read the poem, *Children Learn What They Live*, but we had learned what our parents lived and managed, in some small way, to pass it on. As Dorothy Law Nolte says,

> If a child lives with criticism,
> he learns to condemn.
> If a child lives with hostility,
> he learns to fight.
> If a child lives with fear,
> he learns to be apprehensive....
> If a child lives with encouragement,
> he learns to be confident....

Of course, encouragement is not just for parents and children, or grandparents and grandchildren, for that matter. We may not have the influence on others we have upon those with whom we live, but everyone needs encouragement. Everyone needs a cheer-leader. Everyone needs approval, recognition and praise.

Which makes me wonder: why have I not become a better encourager, not just to my children, but to my colleagues at work, to my friends, even the people I meet?

While walking through my neighborhood one day, I found myself admiring a house along the way. It was a humble home, single story, one-car garage, painted white with gray trim. But it was well appointed and immaculately maintained. The grass was carefully mown, the shrubs neatly trimmed, even the windows sparkled. Then I noticed the owner, an elderly lady, working in the yard (as you might expect). When I said, "Your home looks beautiful," she beamed with delight. Why don't I do that kind of thing more often?

I know a man who writes three notes of encouragement every week. Not long letters, just little notes. But those notes feel big to the people who receive them. Three notes a week, fifty-two weeks a year; that's one hundred and fifty-six acts of encouragement every year, more than fifteen hundred in a decade. It has been years since that wise man told me about his simple practice, and I have yet to make writing notes of encouragement a personal discipline. But I know how good it feels to hear those words, how it lifts the spirit and inspires one to keep going.

"Go Gramps, Go! You can do it!"

Chapter Five

"Silly Gunkle"

The title of this chapter needs some explanation. Not the 'silly' part. Everyone knows what the word silly means. But what is a 'Gunkle'? Believe it or not, a Gunkle is a Great Uncle. 'G' for Great and 'unkle' for Uncle, since Guncle, when written, looks rather French and might be pronounced by the uninformed as Gun-cle`. And Silly Gunkle is anything but a Gun-cle`. Silly Gunkle is Naomi's favorite Great Uncle, my wife's sister's husband who goes by the name of Chris in normal society. But to Naomi he is simply Gunkle, or Silly Gunkle, when he does something a bit strange, which happens rather often in Naomi's presence.

It is amazing the things people will do to attract the attention of a child. We have all seen it, and most of us in our less guarded moments have done it: made a silly face, let strange noises slip from our lips or started a peek-a-boo game we hoped no one would catch on a candid camera. There is just something about the challenge and pleasure of connecting with a little child that makes us throw caution to the wind and do things we would not normally do. But Silly Gunkle has refined this act of daring to an art.

I wish I could show you on video. Actually, I wish I had caught him on video because the blackmail would be lucrative. But I did not catch him, and even if I had I could not put the video in print. So you will just have to use your imagination. Imagine someone with unusual control of his facial expressions, say a pantomime artist. Then picture that mime as a comedian who is willing to cross normal boundaries of decorum to see a child laugh. That is Silly Gunkle. If you are still drawing a blank, maybe a cross between Charlie Chaplin, Groucho Marx and the Three Stooges would give you an idea of what I mean.

Whatever you call the strange expressions Chris makes or the unexpected moves of his head, neck and hands, Naomi loves them, and she loves her Gunkle for doing them. She also likes to imitate him, which elevates the importance of what Gunkle does to a whole new level. It is one thing, you see, to laugh at a circus clown in the ring, but it is another to want to become that clown at home. Fortunately, Gunkle does not do anything questionable, just strange, and at this stage in Naomi's life doing things that are strange is usually cute, especially to her family. In fact, we have spent hours laughing at the expressions Naomi makes as she does what she saw her Gunkle do, while saying out loud, "Silly Gunkle, Silly Gunkle."

But lately I have been thinking about the power of what takes place between Naomi and her Gunkle. As I thought about it, a song came floating back into my mind from somewhere in the seventies:

> My child arrived just the other day.
> He came to the world in the usual way,
> But there were planes to catch,
> and bills to pay.
> He learned to walk while I was away,
> And he was talking before I knew it,
> and as he grew he said,
> "I'm gonna be like you, Dad,
> You know I'm gonna be like you."

Cat's in the Cradle begins innocently enough. There is even a catchy nursery rhyme chorus.

> The cat's in the cradle and the silver
> spoon,
> Little boy blue and the man in the moon.
> When you comin' home, Dad?
> I don't know when,
> But we'll get together then, Son,
> You know we'll have a good time then.

But before long the words of this song begin to hurt.

> My son turned ten just the other day.
> He said, "Thanks for the ball, Dad,
> come on let's play.
> Can you teach me to throw?"
> I said, "Not today,
> I got a lot to do." He said "That's okay."
> And then he walked away,
> but his smile never dimmed.
> He said, "I'm gonna be like him, yeah,
> You know I'm gonna be like him."

This is the story of a father who doesn't have time for a son who loves and admires him. In the final verse this sad song becomes downright haunting, and when the chorus changes the order of two little words—dad and son—the message is unforgettable.

> I've long since retired,
> my son's moved away.
> I called him up just the other day.
> I said, "I'd like to see you
> if you don't mind."
> He said, "I'd love to Dad
> if I could find the time.
> You see, my new job's a hassle
> and the kids have the flu.
> But it's sure nice talking to you, Dad,
> It's sure been nice talking to you."

> As I hung up the phone
> it occurred to me,
> He's grown up just like me,
> My boy was just like me.

> The cat's in the cradle and the silver
> spoon,
> Little boy blue and the man in the moon
> When you comin home, Son?
> I don't know when,
> But we'll get together then, Dad,
> You know we'll have a good time then.

Children are born imitators. Like little mirrors they reflect the lives of those around them, especially those closest to them. It is no mystery why I love baseball or fishing. At the age of five, I was standing in front of a full length mirror watching my father pitch so I could imitate him. By six I was throwing and he was catching most evenings in the back yard. Then every summer we packed the poles and tackle boxes in the truck and headed north to Oregon to fish for trout in Crater Lake or salmon in the bay. I can still remember watching a young boy play a forty pound king salmon for thirty minutes from my perch in the boat next to him. My dad's excitement was contagious as that majestic fish leaped completely out of the water and shook its head to break free from the line.

Children become what they hear and see, and much more is learned through imitation than formal instruction—which makes me glad Gunkle does more than make silly faces. He also is an accomplished musician. Every Sunday after church when Mommy brings Naomi into the sanctuary, the first thing she wants to do is see Gunkle, and Gunkle is always up on the platform with the musical instruments. But as soon as Naomi comes near, Gunkle stops what he is doing and takes her by the hand, to the drums or guitars or whatever instrument draws her attention. Then he sits down with her and lets her play. He even shows her how.

Because Naomi loves her Gunkle she wants to do what he does. So perhaps one day she will play lead guitar in a worship band, or piano in a concert hall, or in her living room. Now that wouldn't be so silly, would it?

Chapter Six

"Baby Yesus"

I am sure my wife thought my senses had left me under the strain, and perhaps she was right. I was working the night shift at a gas station to make ends meet while spending the days trying to finish my doctoral dissertation. Our girls were quite young, Sarah five and Rachel eight, and we lived in a tiny six hundred square foot apartment at the back of another family's property, which the generous owners allowed us to use in exchange for work. I hate to admit it, but we were so poor our girls qualified for subsidized lunches at school. So yes, I was under stress.

But that afternoon we were taking a break. My dad, who bought and sold antiques for a hobby, had invited us to an auction, and since we thought it would be fun, we took him up on the offer. The only problem was that there was a Hummel nativity set at the auction, and for some reason which I could never adequately explain to my wife, I had always wanted a Hummel nativity. Oh, and did I mention, it was Christmas time?

So when the auctioneer started the bidding I raised my hand. At first my wife ignored me, hoping the problem would go away. But when I did it a second time she looked over at me with that "Are you crazy?" look in her eyes. But apparently I was crazy, because I kept raising my hand as the price went higher and higher, and before I knew it (or my wife could stop me) I had spent more money on that set of foreign figurines than we set aside for our entire Christmas.

Oddly enough, I have never regretted that purchase. Every Christmas since, and there have been more than twenty, we slowly unwrap each and every precious piece and carefully place it on the mantel. Then, almost daily during the season I look at the holy scene. Sometimes I focus on a shepherd or a wise man, sometimes on Mary or Joseph. But every time I look at that nativity I always see the same thing.

I see every eye fixed on Jesus. I see knees bowed, faces turned, heads bent, and everyone looking his way. Even the animals seem to join in this implicit act of worship. Now I know that most nativities are historically inaccurate. History teaches us, for example, that the wise men (court astrologers from some eastern kingdom) were not even present when the babe was born. But that does not really matter, at least not as much as having them there. The wise men need to be at the nativity so we can tell the story, and even more importantly, they need to be there so they can offer their gifts and join in the worship.

Even a child knows that. Or perhaps I should say, even a child can teach us that.

It was Christmas, 2009, and we were unwrapping our Hummel nativity for the nineteenth time, arranging it with care on the slate mantel above our fireplace. It was the first Christmas Naomi was old enough to understand what was happening. She had lived through one other yuletide, but at eight months of age, opening presents was more about the wrapping paper than the gift, and the nativity on the mantle could have been a hundred miles away for all she cared. But not this year.

This year, almost as soon as Naomi walked into the room, she noticed the nativity. Walking up to the fireplace, her eyes fixed on the mantel, she held up her little arms and said, "Hug, hug," which you already know means, "Pick me up, please." So I scooped her into my arms and lifted her eye level with the mantel. Pointing her finger at the figure in the center she said in an excited voice, "Baby Yesus. Baby Yesus."

"Yes, that's baby Jesus," I said. "And that's his mommy, Mary." Then I started to tell Naomi about the other figures gathered round. But she was not interested. She had eyes for only one.

"Tousch, tousch," she said. She wanted to touch baby Jesus. So gently I picked him up and let her touch him. Then I put him back on the mantle.

However, that was only the beginning. Every time Naomi came to our house that December she would do the same thing. She would walk over to the fireplace and say, "Baby Yesus, Baby Yesus." Then she would lift her arms in the air and cry, "Hug, hug" until one of us picked her up and let her tousch "Baby Yesus."

This year the ritual has taken a new turn. Naomi no longer lifts her arms and says, "Hug." She is way past that. Now if she wants to see baby Jesus she simply says, "Pick me up, please." But there has been another change in our house as well. We wanted Naomi and her little brother to become more personally involved in the Christmas story. So we bought a "Little People" nativity set. Needless to say, that one is even more historically challenged than the Hummel figurines. But it has one great advantage: you can play with it.

So one day I walked into our great room, the one with the fireplace and nativity mantel, and what did my wondering eyes behold? Our busy granddaughter had taken all the Little People—Mary and Joseph, wise men and shepherds, the camel, donkey, and sheep, all of them—and made them face baby Jesus. Now let me draw a picture for you. They were not facing Jesus the way the Hummel figurines were facing Jesus, carefully placed at the appropriate distances to give the proper aesthetic effect. Not at all. They were pushed into the stable as close as they could get, piled in, if you will, like a crowd of children pressing their noses against the glass of a candy store, perhaps like the crowds used to press in upon Jesus when he walked the earth.

It was the perfect cartoon version of what the nativity is all about. Now keep in mind, I have never told my budding theologian about my interpretation of nativities. She just knew, instinctively, intuitively, wisely, like a child. It is just what the story is about: every knee bowed, every face turned, every eye on Jesus.

Naomi is just a little girl. When she grows up she will have to make her own decisions about what she believes and whose teaching she will follow. She will encounter, as I have, and I am sure you have too, a baffling array of opinions and interpretations; and she will do so, unlike her grandfather, in a world that finds it increasingly difficult to believe any large-scale truth claims. But I hope one truth goes down deep. I hope it becomes her instinctive reaction to the challenges of life. There is room for debate and difference of opinion about many things in the Christian religion, but not this. To be a Christian is to keep Jesus at the center, the still, small point around which all our thinking, all our believing, all our living turns.

Oh, did I tell you what Naomi said to her mother the other day, a week or so after I found all her little people and animals nosing in to see Jesus? She said, "Mommy, Jesus is a King."

Chapter Seven

"Tousch"

I have already told you that Naomi likes to "tousch," at least she likes to touch the Baby Jesus on our fireplace mantle. But the Hummel figurine of Jesus is not the only thing Naomi wants to "tousch." She wants to touch Mary and Joseph, and the wise men, too, especially the beautiful dark skinned one. She wants to touch flowers and leaves, and tea cups sitting on shelves. She wants to touch Calvin, our poodle, and Lucy, her own not-so-friendly cat. She wants to touch the brass kaleidoscope on our end table and the books on Gramps' bookcase and the spoon MiMi is using to cook supper. She doesn't just want to touch them, she wants to hold them and look through them and stir with them. In fact, "tousch" may be one of Naomi's favorite words, because touching is one of the most important ways she connects with her world.

But our granddaughter, I would venture to say, is not unique in this. Human beings as a species are inclined to touch. In the case of children, touching seems to be a form of exploration. They do not really know what something is until they know what it feels like, and they don't know that until they touch it or put it in their mouths, which is just a sloppier, more intimate kind of touching.

But this learning through touch is not something that ends the day we stop putting things in our mouth. I will never forget the feel of my grandfather's sandpaper cheek, or the smell of Old Spice which accompanied that touch. How about you? Can you remember mud squishing through your toes or rain falling on your face and into your open mouth? How about the feel of the sun on a warm summer day or the touch of your first kiss? We human beings are tactile creatures. We live and learn through our senses and the sense of touch, though sometimes taken for granted, is the most sensual of our senses.

So we touch, not only to explore and learn; we touch for pleasure. That is why, for example, I refuse to read my books on a Kindle. There is just something about the pleasure of turning pages that makes a screen sterile by comparison. I even collect old books, especially leather bound volumes, because nothing looks and feels quite like old leather. I do not like to wear gloves when working in the yard for the same reason. I want to feel the grain of the wood and the grit of the sand on my skin. Besides, I can't get a good grip through the false skin of a pair of gloves.

So we touch to experience the fullness of what life has to offer, and I imagine our granddaughter Naomi wants to touch for the same reason. But here is the question that keeps running through my mind: Why does Noami ask permission? When Naomi points to something and says, "Tousch," she is saying, in effect, "I want to touch that. May I?" Well, why doesn't she just reach out and touch it, or grab it and go as most two year old children would?

To what do I attribute this surprising tendency to ask permission? Perhaps her parents have simply done a superior job training their daughter in the etiquette of making requests. But when I look at Naomi's younger brother, who is being raised by the same mother and father, I do not notice the same polite hesitancy. No. This one barrels full steam ahead, touching this and grabbing that, more inclined to seek forgiveness than ask permission. So there must be more in Naomi's case than parental training.

As I pondered my granddaughter's behavior one day, a thought occurred to me. Touching is a rather risky business, isn't it? When you reach out to touch you do not know what you will find at the end of your finger tip. It might be so hot it burns, or so cold it stings. It might slip from the hand and break, or the mere touch of it may cause the big people in one's life to raise their voices in a frightening way—which makes touching a lot like the rest of life. As Bilbo Baggins once said to his nephew, "It's a dangerous business, Frodo, going out your door."

Perhaps Naomi's little request, "Tousch?" is a recognition of that risk. She is, after all, a careful and sensitive child, and displeasure on the faces of the big people in her life, when vigorously expressed, can be frightening. It makes her feel like she might be doing something dangerous—and she may be. After all, who knows better than the big people in one's life what can hurt and what is safe?

There is an ancient story in the Bible about touching. Perhaps you remember it. Adam and Eve had been placed by God in the Garden of Eden and invited to enjoy all the good things their Creator had made, with one exception. They could not eat from one tree in the middle of the garden.

That tree was called by the storyteller "the tree of the knowledge of good and evil," which is a rather strange name for a tree, until one ponders its significance. You see, if Adam and Eve had trusted God enough to obey His prohibition, they would have known only good, not evil. But when they reached out to pick that forbidden fruit, to touch it, if you will, the bitter taste of evil became a personal experience, and God's Garden was forever lost.

What a difference it might have made if, on the day of her temptation, Eve had pointed to that fateful fruit and asked her Creator, "May I Touch?" I guess what I am suggesting is that Naomi's little request may reflect one of life's great questions. "Will this be good or bad for me?"

So how do we respond when our grand-daughter turns to us and says, "Tousch"? We do what we would imagine God doing. We give her a garden full of Yeses. When Noami says "Tousch" we say "Yes" as often as we can. We say yes to the Hummel figurine. We say yes to Calvin (even though he is not sure what to make of this little intruder). We say yes to flowers and kaleidoscopes and serving spoons, even gorilla statues. We want our precious Naomi to experience all that life has to offer, all that is good and beautiful and true, everything rough and smooth and curly and straight. We want her to explore, to take risks and to enjoy life, to learn that stepping out her front door in not just dangerous, but wild and wonderful as well. So we say, "Yes, yes!"

But sometimes we say "No."

"No, honey, you cannot touch MiMi and Gramps' Navajo Wedding Vase. It's fragile, and if it broke, we would be very sad." Nor do we remove the vase from her reach, because we believe it is important for Naomi to learn to honor the boundaries set by the wise people in her life. Hopefully, when she grows up she will still honor those boundaries, at least the boundaries that keep her safely walking the path to what is good.

Chapter Eight

"Puback"

This one caught me by surprise. Maybe it shouldn't have, but it did, and it took some reflection to realize that my granddaughter is a lot like me. It was many Thursdays ago when Naomi first looked up and saw my duck. No, not a little yellow rubber duck; a fairly large black wooden duck. It is an old decoy carved by some unknown craftsman in the Susquehanna River Valley which I received as a gift one Christmas. I have it carefully placed on the top of the bookshelf above my desk. I like it there. It suits me.

But one Thursday Naomi wanted it. So she pointed up and said, you guessed it, "Tousch."

For a moment I hesitated, but then I more wisely said, "OK, Honey, let me get it down."

While I was doing that she pointed to another bird sitting up and away, a much smaller carving of a goose. So I brought that one down, too, and for ten minutes Naomi played happily with my two wooden friends.

But none of that was a surprise. What surprised me is what she did when she was done playing. She handed me the duck and said, "Puback. Puback." She wanted me to put the duck back where I got it, and then the goose as well. Since that day Naomi has done the same thing almost every Thursday she visits. She has walked into my study, pointed first to the duck, then the goose, and asked me to bring them down. Then after playing for a while she wants me to put them back— exactly where they were.

Those are not the only two objects she wants me to "puback." That may have been the first time I noticed, but since then I have become aware of how often Naomi says "puback" after she says "tousch." In fact, I would say it has become a pattern. She wants to play with something that is out of reach, something that does not belong to her and is not a toy. Then after playing, she wants it put back just the way it was.

Maybe that's because she wants to make sure those things are there next time she comes to play; or maybe she wants Gramps to know she can be trusted with something as special as his favorite duck or goose. Or maybe, just maybe, there is something else going on.

Sometimes when my wife calls me "Honey" I wince. I usually like that term of endearment, but when she says it in a certain tone, with a recognizable hesitation and characteristic change in pitch, I say to myself, "Oh no, here it comes."

"Huu-ney," she calls, "Can you come here for a moment?"

"Why, Dear? What do you want?"

"Well, I want to move something—just a few things. It won't be so bad. You'll like it, I'm sure."

My dear wife adds those last two sentences because she knows how much I hate to rearrange the furniture in our house. It's not the work of moving things around that bothers me. I would do that in a heartbeat. It is the change itself I find difficult. I like things the way they are. I am used to sitting in this recliner on this side of the room looking out that window and seeing that particular view, and I do not see any good reason why it should change. I know that may sound silly, especially if you are an interior designer, or anyone who likes change, for that matter. But I don't.

Neither does my little Naomi apparently. She likes her routines. She likes to eat the same foods; she likes to follow the same bedtime rituals; she likes to read the same books over and over again. She also wants things "puback" the way they were. She is a child after my own heart.

Now I know there is no real virtue in resisting my wife's creative urges. She needs the opportunity to explore and create as much as I do, and her home is one place where she can do that. But may I also say, there is something good about things staying the way they are? It is called stability—and stability breeds security, and security is often the soil in which confidence grows. In fact, people who take risks often do so because they have managed to develop a real and rooted sense of security.

That is one of the reasons why Cindi and I hope to stay put until our grandchildren are grown. Not only do we need the benefit of a stable home and enduring friends and consistent labor in the same field, but our granddaughter Naomi and her little brother, Noah, need stability too. When they grow up we want them to step out their front door and go on grand adventures, and we hope growing up with MiMi and Gramps, and in a community of stable friends, will help them find the courage and confidence to do so.

Come to think of it, I believe I will leave my duck to Naomi in my will. Better yet, I'll give it to her when she buys her first home, and write these words on the bottom: *Puback. We like things just the way they are.* Or maybe, *From strong roots tall trees grow.*

Love, Gramps.

Chapter Nine

"No, I Don't"

My wife suffers from fibromyalgia, a chronic and painful condition which affects every aspect of her life. Activities that most people find routine, like cleaning the house or carrying a child, can lead to days of aching pain; and when the pain keeps her awake at night, which it often does, her body is not able to restore itself and the aching persists. The truth is, Cindi is always in pain to one degree or another, and sometimes she even winces when I reach out to touch her. Chronic pain can create other problems, too, like fatigue, irritability, even mild depression. As one fibromyalgia sufferer told her doctor when he suggested she was depressed, "Well, of course I am depressed; I am in pain all the time."

So Cindi has learned the hard way she must set boundaries. She must say, "No." But that is easier said than done, especially when the things that cause pain are so mundane. How do you say "No" to a granddaughter who is lifting her arms crying, "Hug, hug"? You also don't say "No" to working in the garden, if that is what gives you delight, or cleaning your home, if that is where you live. It is simply not possible for people with fibromyalgia to say "No" to everything that causes pain. So what they learn to do is say "No" to the most difficult tasks in order to make space for the more important things in life. They learn, by painful trial and error, what they can and cannot do, and if they are wise, they accept those limits and do their best to live within them.

That would be a whole lot easier if the people around them understood. But we do not. We look at them and they look fine. Then we look at the things we want them to do and those activities don't seem hard to us. So we grow frustrated with their pain and try, sometimes directly but more often subtly and indirectly, to push them beyond their limits. "Come on, Hon, the drive is not that long. We really should go." Or, "Let's have everyone over to our house. It won't take that much to get ready." At least, that is what I did for years. Alas, *ve get too soon oldt undt too late schmart.*

But I am slowly learning that it is a good thing to live within limits, which is a hard lesson for someone who thinks of himself as being able to do whatever needs to be done. It is also a hard truth to practice as a pastor. Contrary to popular opinion a pastor works more than one day a week. In fact, sixty hours is standard fare, and the boundaries between work and personal life are sometimes so thin that it is difficult to determine where private life ends and public service begins. So my wife's struggle with chronic pain has become a life lesson for me as well, and finally I am learning to "just say No."

"No, I don't think I'll serve on that committee."

"No, I don't believe I will rearrange my schedule to meet with him."

"No, I will not leave my family tonight."

So perhaps you can imagine the pleasure I experience when I hear my granddaughter Naomi say, "No, I don't." Of course, that may have something to do with the way she says it. Most two year olds say "No" quite often, and according to child psychologists, they need to. They are discovering their wills and developing a necessary sense of independence, even if it is frustrating for their parents at times. But oddly enough, Naomi doesn't say, "No" very often. What she says instead is, "No, I don't."

"Do you want to sit in your high chair to eat lunch?"

"No, I don't." She prefers to use the big people's stool and sit at the counter.

"Do you want to read *The Cat in the Hat*?"

"No, I don't." Then she picks up another volume of *Frog and Toad*.

"Do you want some of this tasty chicken MiMi made?"

"No, I don't." She would rather eat fruits and vegetables (seriously).

Now you have to admit, there is something more appealing about "No, I don't," spoken with a small, lilting voice, than a short, loud and aggressive "No!" It makes you stop and listen more carefully—at least it has that effect on me. It also makes me wonder, "Is there any good reason to counter this assertion of will?"

Usually the answer is, "No, there isn't." Children need the freedom to make choices, to express and even sometimes assert their wills. Of course, they also need to learn to obey their parents and care about the needs and desires of others. But they do not need to be controlled by those desires and certainly not manipulated, which makes me think of another episode in Naomi's young life.

This one occurred while she was visiting her GiGi, which is her great grandmother on her MiMi's side. Grantie and Gunkle were there, as well as Naomi's Mommy and Auntie Sarah, all card carrying members of my wife's hugging relatives. So when it came time for Mommy to take Naomi home for her nap, she was encouraged to make the rounds and give everyone a kiss 'n hug. But for some reason she did not want to kiss 'n hug GiGi that day. Mommy encouraged her to do so, but when Naomi resisted she wisely let it go. Hugs and kisses are not something to be forced.

But GiGi would not let it go. She followed Mommy out to the car and when Naomi was buckled into her seat, GiGi leaned in to get that coveted kiss 'n hug. Naomi turned away. Once again, that should have been the end of it. But GiGi was determined to get her good-bye kiss. So she started rubbing her eyes with her hands, and in a weepy voice moaned, "You will make GiGi cry!"

Without missing a beat, our little Naomi looked straight ahead and said, "Just don't get my car seat wet." That was the end of that (except for the hours of laughter we have enjoyed remembering that moment).

Now I hope Naomi grows up to be a caring, sensitive human being who sincerely loves people and seeks to meet their needs. But that is not the same thing as being controlled or manipulated by them. People need personal boundaries. They need to be able to make their own decisions about what is required of them and what they are able to do. They need the freedom to say, "No, I don't."

Of course they also need to be able to say, "Yes, I do," which is what Naomi *always* says when her Mommy asks, "Do you want to give Gramps a kiss 'n hug?"

Chapter Ten

"I'm Helping"

Where does it go? That's what I want to know. It is winter now, but this past fall, our back yard was covered with leaves, at least in the places where deciduous trees grow. Fortunately most of our property is planted in pine, so raking autumn leaves is not an all day task. But it is a job that needs to be done and Thursday was as good a time as any to get it done. So I put on my coat and gloves and headed outside.

Of course Naomi wanted to go with me; and she didn't just want to go with me. She wanted to do what I was doing. She wanted to wear a coat because Gramps was wearing a coat, and she wanted to put on her boots and gloves when Gramps put on his. Then, as I started raking, she wanted to do that too.

The moment I will never forget, though, is when we were bending over picking up leaves to put in the bag. Suddenly she looked up at me with those beautiful blue eyes and said, "I'm helping." It was such a happy, satisfied look, I felt like picking her up and swinging her round and round for joy.

But what I want to know is: Where does that go? Where does that happy, satisfied look of contentment in the work of raking autumn leaves go when a child becomes an adult? I am no expert, since I have only two grandchildren, and both are so exceptional they may not be representative of the human race. But it seems to me that little children find more pleasure in some forms of work than adults do.

Naomi, at least, loves to help. She wants to help MiMi fix dinner. She wants to help Gramps rake leaves or pick up the little 'presents' our toy poodle leaves behind (that's a tricky one). Sometimes she even wants to help pick up her toys (except when it means she has to go to bed). And when Naomi is helping she likes to say so.

"Can I help?" she asks MiMi.

"I'm helping," she says to Gramps.

"I helped," she happily announces to Mom when she gets home.

Work for Naomi is helping. It is doing something *for* someone she wants to please and *with* someone she loves. In fact, if someone is not with her then Noami's willingness to work is rather short lived. Picking up blocks or books by herself is simply not something she is motivated to do. But helping MiMi or Gramps pick up the blocks or books is done with a smile on her face and a cheerful "I'm helping" on her lips (most of the time). So maybe that is the answer to the question, "Where does the pleasure go?" Does the joy of work disappear when it is no longer done for or with someone?

Not entirely, I hope. There is a kind of pleasure and contentment that comes from work well done in and of itself. An artist, for example, takes pleasure in her ability to express herself and a craftsman is satisfied by the excellence of his own creation. In fact, I would hope that in some important sense, work is its own reward. Work is the way human beings do what we think is good, create what we feel is beautiful and express what we believe is true.

But I wonder: was work ever meant to be done alone, truly alone? I take personal pleasure in keeping the yard well groomed. But I take even more pleasure in the yard when my wife is pleased with it or my family and friends enjoy a picnic on it, or when the neighbors are proud to have me in the neighborhood because of it. Even more to the point, I find it easier to work in the yard—less tiring, more satisfying—when someone is by my side. In other words, my work is most satisfying and sustainable when I do it for others and with others, when it is a form of helping. Just like Naomi.

Maybe that is why modern work has become so hard. People don't see themselves as helping each other anymore. They have become cogs in a wheel producing widgets for people they will never see and profits for investors they will never know. It is all so impersonal. Often work is done in front of a solitary computer in the loneliness of a cubicle. There may be relationships in the office, but people don't work together anymore. The company may be serving a good purpose, but we don't see the results. We are not helping each other do good things for other people. We have lost sight of this personal purpose.

For little children, the line between work and play is blurred. Play is their work and their work is often play. That is partly because no one is depending on them for their daily bread and they really don't have to do what they do. Life is simpler for a child. But I believe work can become more playful and joyful for adults than it often is. Just think of an Amish barn raising. The work is hard and the day is long, but there is joy in the labor because these men, women and children are helping people they know and love, and they are doing it together.

When the dinner bell rings they all gather for a celebratory meal. Though preparing the meal was hard work, and those who sit down together are weary from physical labor, the lines between work and play have been blurred by the love of a community. Some of their fondest memories are these hard and happy work days together.

We are not Amish, and it is more difficult in our modern world to work together or to see how our work helps people we love. Nor are we children any more. People do depend on the work we do for their daily bread. But helping still makes us happy, or at least it can. Maybe that happy, satisfied look on Naomi's face doesn't have to go away after all; and maybe, just maybe, I can learn to find more pleasure and contentment in my daily chores by doing them with and for others.

Chapter Eleven

"Where Moon?"

Goodnight Moon is one of those special childhood books that has charmed children to sleep for years, and like many other boys and girls, Noami has a copy of it on her bookshelf. So perhaps that was the reason why she first asked the question. Or maybe it was her way of connecting with Great Aunt Melanie when she visited the September Naomi turned a year and half old. Whatever the reason, here is what happened.

Looking out the window late one morning, Aunt Melanie spied a full moon lying low in the sky, an unusual sight that time of day. So she called Naomi over and with a tone of excitement in her voice, "Look, Naomi, the moon. Do you see the moon?"

Apparently she did, and it made an impression, because after her nap that day Naomi walked over to the same window and turning, with her palms held up in a questioning gesture, asked Melanie, "Where Moon? Where Moon?" Nor was that the last time we heard this question.

Not only did she ask it "again, again" the same day, even after the moon had faded from view, but a week or so later, when I was driving Naomi to our house for another Thursday with MiMi and Gramps, the same question arose. "Where Moon?" she asked from her car seat in the back. I tried to explain that the moon wasn't in the sky today, and that it usually comes out at night. But Naomi just kept asking. After all, she had seen it in the daytime before. Why couldn't she see it again?

For months afterward the question kept coming. "Where Moon?" she would ask when we were driving. "Where Moon?" she would say as she looked out the window of our house. "Where Moon?" she would ask Mommy at home.

Sometimes the moon was there and we could point to it. "There it is," we would say.

But other times, for reasons only an adult can understand, we would have to say, "No, Honey, you can't see the moon right now. It isn't here."

That must be a hard thing for a child of two to understand. Why would something as beautiful and exciting as the moon be here one day and gone the next? Why could you see it at one moment, but not another? When would Naomi understand that the presence and absence of the moon is determined by the turning of the earth and the location of the sun?

"Philosophy," Socrates declared, "begins in wonder." The search for understanding which penetrates beyond simple observation begins in a moment of confusion. Why are things not as I expect them to be? Why is the moon not here? Where has it gone?

I am sure that natural philosophy (now called science) is well beyond the limits of my little Naomi's mind. But making sense of her world is not. In fact, from the earliest days, I have been watching her young mind work. Our first game, which quickly became my favorite, was the pointing game. Before she could even walk, I would hold Naomi in my arms and start pointing. I would point up to an object on the ceiling and say, "light." I would point down at our poodle with its wagging tail and say, "Calvin." I would point out the window and say "tree" or "bird" or "grass". She loved it. In fact, soon Naomi started pointing herself and waiting for me to say the word. Then we would go from room to room and window to window pointing to one thing after another until I was tired of the pointing game. Eventually, of course, she learned to say the words herself and the game faded away.

Naomi was making sense of her world. She was learning what things were by learning what to call them. Soon one word names gave way to two word sentences, then two words became three, and three became six, until the process of describing and explaining her world through the marvel of human language was well under way. Now instead of pointing to an object and asking its name, Naomi brings me a book and says, "Read to me." Stories have taken the place of simple words and sentences. But "Where Moon?" will always be for me a picture of my inquisitive grand-daughter's hunger to understand her world.

Isn't it amazing how our deepest yearnings surface before we turn three years of age, and they surface in a form without guile? "Hug, Hug," Noami says, because she needs to be loved, "Tousch," because she wants to experience, "Puback," because she yearns for security. "I'm helping," she says, because she wants to do something important with others. "I'm sorry, Gramps," she confesses, because she needs to stay connected to someone she loves. "No, I don't" and "Yes, I do" bear witness to Naomi's emerging need to express her will and draw personal boundaries. Even "Silly Gunkle" and "Baby Yesus" are manifestations of fundamental human needs, the need to imitate and the need to worship. Now Naomi asks, "Where Moon?"

If she will follow that question it will lead her, like the ancient mariner and modern scientist before her, on a journey of discovery without limit, but not without purpose, for to understand the world, and her place in it, is as basic a need as the need for love, security or significance. We need to know that the world makes sense. We need to understand where the moon has gone and when we can count on it coming back again. Otherwise, our world will be as unpredictable and wobbly as a ship at sea in a storm at night—and no one likes the way that feels.

But I cannot shake the sense that I have not yet exhausted the significance of my little granddaughter's rather big question. "Where Moon?" spoken by a two year old, arms lifted and palms turned up, with a quizzical wrinkle on her brow, is an unforgettable and endearing expression of the human hunger to understand. But the moon is not quite like the other things Naomi and I named when we played our pointing game. Trees and bushes, butterflies and bees, flower petals and bright green grass are all quite amazing and full of wonder and delight.

But the moon, that's something special. It can't be touched, it can't be tasted, it can't be taken in one's hand or climbed branch by branch. No, it's up there, far away. When I look at the moon I am gazing up into the sky, and the sky, especially at night, with its stars twinkling in the blackness, feels like nothing else I have ever seen. Maybe a little like the ocean, or more correctly, the edge of the ocean as it disappears on the far horizon. It feels like forever.

The sky above and the horizon below are perhaps the closest we come as finite human beings to 'seeing' eternity. To gaze at the moon and the stars in the nighttime sky is to be led, almost by force of logic, to ask the deeper questions of life. How do I fit into the vastness of all this? Does everything finally make sense? Or to put it in the words of the ancient psalmist:

> When I consider your heavens,
> the work of your fingers,
> the moon and the stars
> which you have set in place,
> what is man
> that you are mindful of him,
> the son of man
> that you care for him?

Of course, Naomi was not raising these questions when she looked out the window that first morning and asked, "Where Moon?" Not by any stretch of the imagination. But if Socrates was correct, wisdom begins in wonder, and if I am correct, the spirit which looks up into the sky and asks "Where Moon?" is the same spirit that someday will look toward heaven and ask, "Who am I?" and

"Who are You?" May my little Naomi never stop asking such important questions.

Chapter Twelve

"You Don't Smell Good"

My little Naomi comes from a long line of sensitive people, physically sensitive I mean. Her Auntie Sarah, my daughter, could tell at the age of six when we had changed the dishwasher soap just by touching her spoon. She also developed an allergic reaction to cold when she went away to college. Now holding a cold drink in her hand can make her break out. But Sarah comes by her sensitivities honestly. I have struggled all my life with skin allergies; and when Sarah's mother and I went shopping for a new mattress a few years ago, we ended up buying and returning three in a row, all top-of-the-line, until we could find one comfortable enough for my wife to sleep on. Through the process I discovered where the story of "The Princess and the Pea" came from. The Princess must have been one of Naomi's ancient great grandmothers on her MiMi's side.

Now a person cannot really do anything about her physical sensitivity, except learn to deal with it in constructive ways. But I can't help thinking there is some poetic justice in the story my wife told me the other day. While visiting Rachel one afternoon, Cindi watched Naomi approach her mommy, book in hand, and say, "Read to me."

It was a rather long book, and Rachel wanted to visit, so she replied, "Not that one, Honey. It is too long." But Naomi wouldn't take no for an answer. So she turned to MiMi with hopeful eyes and asked, "Will you read to me?"

"Of course I will, Sweetheart." What else is a grandmother to say?

So Naomi crawled up in the chair and snuggled into her lap as MiMi opened the book and began to read. But about half a page into the story, Naomi wrinkled her nose and began to sniff the air, as if she smelled something cooking in the kitchen. She turned to the left and sniffed, then to the right and sniffed, until finally she twisted her head up and around and sniffed in MiMi's direction. That's when she slid off MiMi's lap and down onto the floor.

"You keep reading," Naomi said. "I can hear you from here."

"Why, what's wrong, Honey?" MiMi asked. "Why don't you want to sit in MiMi's lap?"

"You don't smell good, MiMi," she said, wrinkling her nose. Then she repeated, "You keep reading. I can hear you from here."

Of course, MiMi had a better idea. She quickly pulled a mint from her purse, popped it in her mouth and invited her granddaughter back into her lap, so both the snuggling and the story could continue. It probably was a good thing I was not there, because my laughing out loud would have been hard for Naomi to understand. She was, after all, just telling MiMi the truth.

Sounds simple, doesn't it—just telling the truth? Yet how rare it is to find a relationship between adults where people tell each other the truth, the whole truth and nothing but the truth. It is not that we lie. We just don't say everything that needs to be said.

That is one of the many reasons I love my wife. She tells me the truth. She tells me when my breath is bad, which is a good thing, since my job requires me to speak with people face to face. Cindi also carries breath mints in her purse, as much for me as for herself, which is probably why she had one when she needed it for Naomi.

But Cindi tells me more important things than whether my breath could kill. She also tells me when my daughter is feeling neglected or my sermon sounds too harsh, when my life is out of balance or something important is being missed. Cindi even dares to speak into the deepest issues of my heart. She has told me when my life smelled selfish or prideful or insensitive. She has identified blind spots that could have done great damage to myself and others. Though I sing her praises now, sharing those unflattering truths was not always well received. It takes courage to tell someone, even someone you love, there is something wrong in his life.

In fact, it is probably too hard a role for any one person to play in the life of another. So I think we should have more than one person who has the ability and permission to tell us the truth. Cindi and I have some dear friends we have known for over thirty years.

We met them just after we were married, and even though we have traveled all over the country and lived outside the United States for a season, we have managed to stay in touch. They were there when we went through one of the darkest seasons of our lives, and they were also there through many good times.

A few months ago we called them up to see if we could spend the night. Of course they said yes. After enjoying a good meal and catching up, we finally told them the reason for our visit: we wanted to share a painful experience in our lives. It was a tender and difficult evening, because we were opening a soft and wounded part of our souls. But we told them the truth, and they responded with love. They also spoke truthfully in turn. Friendships like that are rare, even priceless.

I realize that all Naomi said to MiMi was "You don't smell good." She was not speaking about the aroma of anyone's soul or pointing to serious personal blind spots. How could she? She is just a child. But Naomi's childlike truth-telling can show all of us a way forward. If we learn to tell each other the truth in little things, like bad breath, then maybe, just maybe, we can learn to speak the truth in bigger things, like hurtful attitudes and painful actions.

But how? What enabled Naomi to tell MiMi she smelled bad, without any sense of fear, and what caused MiMi to respond without resentment or shame? The answer, I think, is obvious. It was love. There is a bond of love between MiMi and Naomi that is not easily threatened. It is certainly not threatened by anything as small as smelly breath.

That is the lesson we need to learn. It is love that enables friends to speak the truth to each other, and it is love that enables them to hear it. The more secure our love, the freer we will be to reveal and to receive the most difficult of truths. Of course, that kind of love is no small thing. It takes many Thursdays to get that deep.

Chapter Thirteen

"Little Brudder"

It just so happened that it was not our Thursday to spend with Naomi. Her other grandparents live nearby, so she spends one Thursday with her MiMi and Gramps and the other with her Grandma and PaPa. We took advantage of this other Thursday to enjoy Naomi's "Little Brudder," Noah, who is every bit as delightful as his big sister. But when the time came for the children to go home, we swung by to pick up Naomi, so her other grandparents didn't have to make the trip. That's when the fun began.

I really do mean fun, because as soon as Naomi got in the car and saw Noah, she squealed with delight. She was thrilled to see him and he was just as happy to see her.

"I missed my Little Brudder!" Naomi cried, and Cindi and I smiled inside.

Then for the next fifteen minutes brother and sister held hands, from one car seat to the next, as three year old Naomi entertained one year old Noah and kept him giggling, like the wee little pig, all the way home. We could hardly believe our eyes and ears.

This joy in each other's company didn't cease when they were carried over the threshold either. As soon as we put them down in their family room they continued to play together, and we thought to ourselves, "Perhaps absence really does make the heart grow fonder."

There was even a point in their play, when Naomi was pushing one of her little bears in a doll stroller, and Noah wanted to do it, too. One stroller, two children, not usually a good combination. But Naomi's mother simply said, "Do you think you could give Noah a turn with the stroller?"

Naomi quickly responded, "Yes, I can" (she really does talk like that) and stepped aside to let her Little Brudder take the handles. We were amazed. But let me tell you how that evening turned out.

Eventually Naomi got tired of letting Noah push her little bear in her stroller, and she wanted them back. So naturally, she took them. Noah, in turn, grabbed the bear and ran into the kitchen, with Naomi hot on his heels. But Noah is a rather determined little guy. So he held on tight and the two of them, for a moment, were locked in a tug-o-war with poor Teddy Bear stretched painfully between. Noah pulled with all his might and Naomi, whether on purpose or not we will never know, let go of little Teddy, and we watched poor Noah fly headfirst into the kitchen cabinet and fall screaming to the floor. That's when MiMi and Gramps decided it was time for grandparents to go home.

That Teddy Bear tug-o-war is a mental picture I will not soon forget. Naomi really does love Noah. She plays with him, she reads to him, she hugs and kisses him, and she sincerely misses him when he is gone. He has become her special partner in life, her "Little Brudder," as she calls him. But Naomi is jealous of the attention Noah receives and sometimes angered by the things he does, especially when what he does keeps her from doing what she wants to do.

I cannot tell you how many times I have seen Naomi watching us as we have focused attention on Noah. Often she will come over, and ask, "What's Noah doin'?" Of course, what she means is, "What is Noah doing that is attracting your attention right now, and will you talk to me instead?" Sometimes she isn't even that subtle. She just says, "Look at me, Gramps! Look at me, MiMi!" as she tries to do something more interesting than her Little Brudder. It is a hard thing to be displaced by another human being, especially one you call your "Brudder."

Let's face it: our brother or sister is our first real experience of a neighbor and our first opportunity to come face to face with the Great Commandment of Jesus, "Love your neighbor as yourself." It sounds so poetic and profound when we hear that verse quoted. But actually doing it, and doing it when we don't feel like doing it, is another matter. Amazing how a tug-o-war between siblings can surface one of life's most fundamental challenges.

To love someone *as* I love myself invites a rather difficult comparison. It invites me to compare two things: my commitment to my own happiness and my commitment to the happiness of another. It also sets a rather high standard. I am to be as interested in what my brother needs, and as committed to meeting those needs, as I am my own needs.

That's quite an expectation, don't you think? It is asking a lot of Naomi to be as committed to her "Little Brudder" receiving attention from MiMi and Gramps as she is to her own desire for that love and attention. It is asking a lot of Naomi to rejoice when her brother rejoices and to be sad when her brother weeps, especially if he is rejoicing over playing with her stroller or weeping over the loss of her Teddy. But that seems to be what Jesus is asking, and it seems to be what love is about.

To love means listening to another person's heart as intently as you listen to your own. It means caring for her needs and looking out for his interests as much or more than your own. In the extreme, it means giving your life for the one you love. "Greater love," Jesus once said, "has no one than this: to lay down his life for his friends." That is the stuff of which love stories are made, the stuff of which the gospel story is made.

Little Naomi, at the tender age of three, is learning how hard it is to truly love her neighbor. What she wants and what he wants is often in tension, and that tension leads to many a conflict. Nor will that tension go away as my little darling grows up. She will feel it when her first girlfriend gets the attention of the boy Noami has set her eyes upon. She will feel it when some of her class mates are more gifted or popular or pretty than Naomi thinks she is. She will even feel it when she gets married, perhaps not at first. Young love has a way of making every sacrifice seem easy. But eventually Naomi will struggle with the tension between her needs and his, his desires and hers; and she will discover it is a tension overcome mostly through the sacrifice of love.

Hopefully, by that time, Naomi will have taken the command of Jesus to heart, because "love your neighbor as yourself" is not just a command. It is the way of life Jesus lived, which gives me hope. If I could learn to live like Jesus then maybe, just maybe, I could experience a measure of his inner life, which means his joy could become my joy, his peace my peace, his love mine as well.

So here is my hope, both for me and my granddaughter: that the tension between our happiness and the happiness of others would eventually fade away, as we find in following Jesus a deeper happiness, the kind that finds joy in the well-being of others. In other words, the joy of love.

Chapter Fourteen

"Oh, The Things She Says!"

After coming this far you could be excused for thinking that this chapter is about Naomi. But it is not. "Oh the things she says!" is actually something we heard over and over again when Naomi's mother was a little girl. You know the saying, "The acorn doesn't fall far from the tree." Well, in the case of our granddaughter that is certainly true. Unfortunately, I was not wise enough in my twenties to write down all of Rachel's little sayings or to reflect upon their significance. But thirty years later I do have some stories to tell.

I could tell you about the danger of putting a ring in one's mouth and the evening we spent at the hospital worrying about what would happen to the one Rachel had just swallowed. Or I could reflect upon the way Rachel named multiple stuffed animals "Christy" because we had forced her to give away her own dog, "Christy," at the tender age of six. Grief is certainly a powerful emotion. But I think the story I will tell is about the time, near age three, when Rachel almost became a thief.

Her mother and her aunt had taken Rachel shopping, and somewhere along the way, in one of the aisles, she had picked up a little stuffed animal. Rachel always had a soft spot for stuffed animals. Still does. But it was a while before Cindi or Lisa discovered the toy, and when they told Rachel she would have to put it back, she was, as you can imagine, quite upset. Rather than make a scene, or push Rachel over an emotional edge, they decided to let her hold the little creature until they finished shopping. Besides, neither mom nor aunt knew where the toy had come from, and Rachel wasn't giving them any clues.

So for the next fifteen or twenty minutes Rachel was happy as a clam and the adults were thankful for the distraction. But eventually the deed had to be done. So when they were paying the bill, Rachel was required, in spite of her many tears, to turn her new found friend over to the nice lady behind the cash register. Then quickly, with some embarrassment, mother and aunt left the store.

Unfortunately, the drama continued through the parking lot, into the car, and all the way home. Little Rachel was beside herself with grief. So Mommy tried to reason with her, reminding Rachel that she had many stuffed animals waiting for her at home. But Rachel would not be consoled. She just "loved" that little creature and kept insisting that she "needed" it.

"I need it!" she cried. "I need it!"

So Mommy proceeded to challenge that idea. "No, Rachel, you do not need it. You have other stuffed animals at home. That stuffed animal does not belong to you. You do not need it. You just want it."

There was a moment of silence. Not complete silence, but wailing gave way to whimpering as Rachel tried to catch her breath and take her mother's words to heart. Then she made a rather startling statement.

Choking back the tears, she said to Cindi, "But Mommy, haven't you ever wanted something so much you felt like you *needed* it?" Yes, Rachel, we have.

In fact, the confusion between need and desire is one of the universal experiences of the human race. "Our hungers drive us," Frederick Forsyth once wrote. Not just our hunger for food, but our hunger for security or significance, our hunger for pleasure or love. The only problem is that our hungers do not always drive us in the right direction. They can lead us to a jar of candy as easily as a well-balanced meal. They can drive us to abuse and addiction as well as to a life of mutual, self-giving love.

Desire by itself is not self-regulating. It makes no judgment about whether what it wants is good or bad, nor can it do so, for desire carries no criteria of discernment within itself. Desire does not know when it wants too much or too intensely, or when it has focused upon the wrong object to satisfy its longing. It simply wants what it wants.

So one of the most important lessons anyone can learn in life is that we do not need to satisfy our desires. In fact, we cannot satisfy all our desires, for they are often in conflict. What we need to do instead is to train our desires to be good followers rather than bad leaders, following what is good instead of leading us to what is bad.

But as my daughter experienced so painfully many years ago, that is easier said than done. In fact, it takes a lifetime of reflection and discipline to do it, reflection on what is really good and the disciplined practice of not doing what we want in order to do what we really need. Not eating everything we desire, but only what makes us healthy; not expressing our sexuality anytime and everywhere, but in the security and intimacy of marriage; not giving in to the desire to get even, but overcoming evil with good; not coveting the teddy bear which belongs to our sister (or her house or car), but being content with what we have.

The incident with the stuffed animal happened more than twenty years ago. Rachel is now a married woman, with children of her own, and one of her most striking, and appealing, qualities is her spirit of calm contentment. She and her husband are just starting out in life. They live in a small, humble two-bedroom duplex, filled with hand-me-down furniture and overflowing with children's toys. Money is so tight that Rachel shops for clothes at consignment stores and gives gifts she makes by hand. But none of that seems to bother her. She and Adam are deeply happy. They have learned the secret of enjoying what they have rather than wanting what they don't. They know the difference between needs and desires.

I have noticed something else as well. When Cindi and I visit our grandchildren in their home, we often find dishes in the sink or laundry sitting in the basket or toys covering the floor. But Rachel does not seem too worried about the mess—because she has made a decision, many decisions, in fact, throughout the day. She has decided to play peek-a-boo instead of washing the dishes; she has decided to read a story to Noah instead of finishing the laundry; she has decided to bake cookies with Naomi rather than clean the house. Rachel has decided to let her lesser duties slide as she does more important things.

But doesn't she *need* to get the laundry done? Doesn't she *need* to keep the house clean? Doesn't she *need* to stay on top of all the chores? No, she does not. She wants to, I am sure, and sometimes she wants to so much she feels like it is a need. But for two decades now Rachel has been learning to distinguish between what she needs and wants, and spending time with her children is more needful, more important, than cleaning the house before her parents come to visit. I guess Rachel has answered her own question, *"Don't you ever feel like you want something so much you think you need it?"* Yes, Honey, but that does not mean you actually do.

Returning
To the Wisdom of the Heart
The Wisdom
of Living in the Present Moment
The Wisdom
of a Simple Hug
The Wisdom
of Believing Wonder
The Wisdom of Childhood

Chapter Fifteen

"Naomi Dance!"

I am not a very good dancer. No, that is not quite true. I am a terrible dancer, the kind of dancer who should stay off the floor and save his partner's toes. I did take lessons, ten ballroom dancing lessons some twenty years ago. But the lessons never took. Maybe the fact that I could not stop counting long enough to feel the rhythm might have had something to do with it. But whatever the reason, my poor wife has to pull me onto the floor at wedding receptions and put up with a less than satisfying partner.

But Naomi *loves* to dance. I don't know when it happened, but early on in her little life Naomi started moving with the music, moving her head, her arms, her legs, and eventually her whole body. Now dancing is one of her favorite things to do, especially when the whole family gathers. She will come into the house and almost immediately ask MiMi to turn the music up so she can start dancing.

I wish you could see it. It is not polished or practiced. It is not synchronized or syncopated. But it is full of energy and life, and it is contagious. Naturally, Naomi insists we join in. "Dance!" she says, and dance we do. MiMi and Gramps dance, Auntie Sarah dances, Gunkle and Grantie dance, G-PaPa dances, even her Little Brudder dances with her.

When I dance with Naomi, I let go. I freely enjoy the moment. I really do. I pick her up and swing her. I imitate the crazy movements of her head and arms and legs. I even add some wild antics of my own (a bit of Silly Gunkle, if you know what I mean). It is not that I have developed any more rhythm or skill in my old age. But it doesn't matter. It is not about the form, and it certainly is not about what others think of me, or even what I think of myself. It's about Naomi.

It is also about setting aside a multitude of inhibitions that normally hold me back. Music and dancing seem to bypass the mind and go directly to the heart. Unfortunately, in much of my life I keep my heart well under the control of my head, so well under control that the heart remains quite hidden and unavailable. Perhaps that is the deeper reason why I never learned to dance well.

But I am learning now. At the ripe old age of fifty-something I am learning to dance. I am being led by my three year old granddaughter onto the floor of life and being asked to let go, to feel the music, to be free and alive and to connect, not through words and ideas alone, but heart to heart through the movement of our bodies to the music. And it is good! To dance with Naomi is to learn the wisdom of uninhibited, heartfelt connection between two human beings who don't need to have it figured out before taking the risk of living.

Obviously, I am not just talking about dancing. Dancing could be a metaphor for much of what this book is about. It is about taking the risk of returning to the wisdom of the heart—the wisdom of living in the present moment, the wisdom of saying, "I'm sorry," the wisdom of a simple hug, the wisdom of telling each other the smelly truth, the wisdom of believing wonder. This book is an invitation to dance the dance of life with all the humility, openness and wonder of a little child.

There is a song by Lee Ann Womack that moves me every time I hear it. It begins softly, "I hope you never lose your sense of wonder," and I think immediately of the child-like wonder I have seen so many times in Naomi's eyes, the wonder at butterflies and bees, floating bubbles and flying birds.

"I hope you still feel small when you stand beside the ocean," LeAnn continues. In other words, I hope you realize how much like a child you really are. "Promise me," she pleads, "that you'll give faith a fighting chance." Dare to look at life through the faith-filled eyes of a child.

Then comes the chorus, rising with pathos and power, "When you get the choice to sit it out or dance," which of course we all do, "I hope you dance...I hope you dance!" That is my wish for you as well. I hope you learn to dance the dance of life with all the humility, openness and wonder of a little child—before you *get too soon oldt.*

I almost hesitate telling you this. It was such a personal moment. But I will risk the disclosure because I so want you to embrace this invitation to dance. One night a few years ago I was alone in the house. Cindi had gone out and our youngest daughter was away at college. So I put a CD in the player and turned the sound way up. By way up I mean I could feel the music in my chest.

It was a collection of worship songs by Rich Mullins, and as he sang I began to sing along, softly at first, but then more boldly. After a while, I rose and began to dance. For an hour or so (actually, I lost track of time) I sang and danced with all my heart as tears fell down my face. I felt like a child in the presence of my Father in heaven.

What I am trying to tell you is that I am finally learning to dance—to be free from the heart, like Naomi, but with the experience of an older and I hope, wiser man.

Chapter Sixteen

"That's the Story of My Teeth"

In 1989 our young family was living in Cambridge, England. The year before we had sold all our earthly belongings and headed out on a grand adventure—exploring the world of Chaucer, Shakespeare, and Beatrix Potter while dad (that's me) studied for his Ph.D. What a life-changing experience that turned out to be! But it was also much lonelier than we had expected. Far removed from family and friends, living in a culture more alien than we anticipated, our minds and hearts often drifted back home. So, in an effort to stay in touch we exchanged videos. We wrote letters, too. But in the days before Skype, a video was the next best thing to being there.

There is one video we recorded that has become a family classic. Six year old Rachel is standing in the family room dressed in a plaid skirt and white blouse, the uniform she had worn that day to her English primary school, and sporting the kind of oversized eyeglasses that were popular in the eighties. Dad had a pair, too. Fortunately, the camera was focused on her, not him.

At first the conversation was like pulling teeth. Rachel couldn't think of anything to say, until Cindi cleverly suggested, "Tell Gramie about your teeth."

That's all it took. Standing there in her school uniform, speaking in the cutest little British accent you can imagine, Rachel told Gramie all about her teeth. Pointing first to one side of the fresh hole in her mouth and then to the other, she carefully explained the history of her missing teeth, from the moment she discovered they were loose to the morning she found quarters under her pillow, left behind, she told us, by the "Tooph Fairy".

But the moment that caused this mono-logue to go down in the annals of family history occurred right at the end. Somehow Rachel managed to narrate most of the tale of her teeth with one or more fingers moving in and out of the gaps in her ivories. But when she was quite finished, she paused, took her fingers out of her mouth, looked straight into the camera and announced, in a rather matter-of-fact manner, "And that's the story of my teeth."

I am not sure why those seven little words struck such a responsive chord in my wife and me. It could have been the charming combination of our daughter's accent, her artful pause and the final turn of phrase, or maybe it was just the completely unexpected nature of the comment. But whatever the reason, that phrase has stuck. It has achieved the status of a proverbial saying in family conversation. Through the years one of us has often told a story about where we have been or what we have done, and then added, with a knowing glance and a memorable rhythm, "And that's the story of my teeth." So, when it came time to finish this book it was almost second nature to add, with a wink and a grin, "and that's the story of my teeth."

Because this book really is the story of my teeth, and my family's teeth, as well. These stories belong to us. They are as personal as the teeth in our mouths, and sometimes just as embarrassing. Not only have you learned that my wife has fibromyalgia, but that I have often been insensitive to her limitations and needs. You know that I don't like my furniture moved, that I can't dance very well, that I tend to be rationally controlled, and that I need hug therapy. Even more humbling, you have seen the way pride has kept me from saying "I'm sorry" and being in a hurry has stolen many precious moments. I have opened my mouth, if you will, and let you look inside. You have seen that the story of my teeth is a very human tale.

But God is not finished with me yet. In fact, the mystery and marvel of my story is that somewhere past mid-life God graced me with grandchildren. As I wrote in chapter two, arriving at a place in life where I could actually see the end of the road, and ponder paths not taken, I received the gift of contemplating the beginning all over again through the eyes of a child. It was not quite like being born again, but almost. I now see more clearly, love more deeply, and enjoy life more fully than I ever did before.

And to think I have only just begun! As a wise man once said in my hearing, "You are an unceasing spiritual being with an eternal destiny in God's great Universe." If Dallas Willard (who spoke those words) is right, and the Bible certainly suggests he is, then we really are like little children on this journey of life. We may indeed grow *too soon oldt and too late schmart* in the seventy or eighty years we walk the earth. But there is more to come, much more; and it is never too late to learn. Never.

So I leave you with a question. What will be the story of your teeth?

Notes

p. 25 Gilbert K. Chesterton, *Orthodoxy* (New York: Image Books, A Division of Doubleday, Garden City, 1959), p.60

p. 32 Ross Campbell, *How to Really Love Your Child* (Colorado Springs: David Cook, 2004).

p. 40 Dorothy Louis Law, "Children Learn What They Live," Torrance Schools Board of Education Newsletter, April 1, 1959.

p. 91 Psalm 8.

Acknowledgments

I would like to thank Jared Reneker for designing the cover, Dan Schmidt for preparing the text, and Doug Waardenburg for bringing the book to print.

But my family deserves the credit for bringing this book to life.

Thank you, Auntie Sarah, for capturing the wisdom of the book in pen and ink. Only those who know Naomi understand how good your illustrations really are.

Thank you MiMi, GiGi, G-PaPa, Gunkle, Grantie, Mommy, Daddy, even Little Brudder for being such good sports and allowing me to tell the story of your teeth.

And thank you, Naomi, for being you. You will always be one of the great loves of my life. I wrote this book for you—and because of you.

But most of all I want to thank my beloved wife, Cindi. This is the story of our teeth, and not a word could have been written without you. What a privilege to share this life and love together!